eclipse

KIRLI SAUNDERS

JOAN

First published in 2025

This project has been assisted by the Australian Government through Creative Australia, its principal arts investment and advisory body.

Joan, an imprint of
Allen & Unwin
Cammeraygal Country
83 Alexander Street
Crows Nest NSW 2065
Australia
Phone: (61 2) 8425 0100
Email: info@allenandunwin.com
Web: www.allenandunwin.com

Allen & Unwin acknowledges the Traditional Owners of the Country on which we live and work. We pay our respects to all Aboriginal and Torres Strait Islander Elders, past and present.

A catalogue record for this book is available from the National Library of Australia

ISBN 978 1 76147 130 8

Cover and internal artwork: Kirli Saunders
Typeset in 11/15 pt Bembo MT Pro by Bookhouse, Sydney
Printed and bound in Australia by the Opus Group

10 9 8 7 6 5 4 3 2 1

MIX
Paper | Supporting responsible forestry
FSC® C001695

The paper in this book is FSC® certified. FSC® promotes environmentally responsible, socially beneficial and economically viable management of the world's forests.

PRAISE FOR

eclipse

'The phenomenal work, spirit, and invitation of Kirli's poetry is a sacred piece of art for the world and truth every person can learn from. Kirli's writing takes every reader on a visionary journey, offering profound insights into the love of blackfullas, the earth we all inhabit, and the enduring power of Aboriginal women . . . a treasure that illuminates the sacred stories and teachings passed down through generations.' **Vanessa Turnbull-Roberts, Bundjalung Widubul-Wiabul woman, human rights advocate, lawyer and writer**

'In this masterpiece collection, Kirli reminds us of the abundance of wisdom each of us can tap into at any time, anywhere, by calling upon our Ancestors. This book is a gift.' **Teela Reid, proud Wiradjuri and Wailwan woman, lawyer, activist and co-founder of Blackfulla Book Club**

'*Eclipse* is ceremony unfurling around us, the invitation into its sacredness a masterful and generous gift.' **Nardi Simpson, award-winning Yuwaalaraay musician and writer**

'*Eclipse* is a necessary testament to the power of storytelling. It reminds us that, in the darkness, there is always light—and that light is the wisdom of the Ancestors, the Old Ways, the strength of community, and the kinship that sustains us.' **Nick Paton, proud Ngunnawal man, journalist with *Koori Mail***

'Everything Kirli Saunders touches, from poetry to a paintbrush, is gold—*Eclipse* is exactly that.' **Narelda Jacobs OAM, Whadjuk Noongar journalist**

Kirli Saunders (OAM) is a proud Gunai Woman who rarely stays in her lane. She's a multi-award-winning multidisciplinary artist, writer, singer-songwriter and consultant. Kirli creates, to connect, to make change, advocating for the land and her communities. She was awarded an Order of Australia Medal for her contribution to the arts (2022). Kirli has partnered with global organisations, including Google, Fender, Sydney Opera House, Qantas, Spotify, Mecca and Aesop on visual art and writing projects.

Her award-winning film collaboration, *Cry of the Glossy* (Grassland Films) has been screened around the world. Kirli created drone installation, *Buungbaa Ma Ndhu* (Fremantle Biennalle × Ngunuggula Gallery) and voice to art digital installation, *TRACES* (Google, Magabala, Sydney Opera House with Kamsani Bin Salleh).

Her eight books include *Returning* (2023), *Afloat* (2024) and *The Land Recalls You* (2024).

Kirli is currently writing *Going Home*, a theatre work with Merrigong, and recording her first album with Mark Harding, in their project, Cooee.

Written on Dharawal & Wadi Wadi with deep reverence for the Elders who've cared for these lands for all times, for my Old People and for all First Nations peoples who cradle this collection in their hands.

Yandingji—my gratitude to you

contents

terrain

in the before time
we cut ancient portals
into spotted gum trunks
to mark the way back to this place
\tap/ \tap/ \tap/
/wriggle chisel
anchored our shape into bark
\tap/
so that our love might
linger *\tap/* longer *\tap/*
than these skin's
\tap/
slid our hands inside her
opening hollow space
to honour
that what was here
in togetherness
was holy
/wriggle chisel
chisel
\tap/

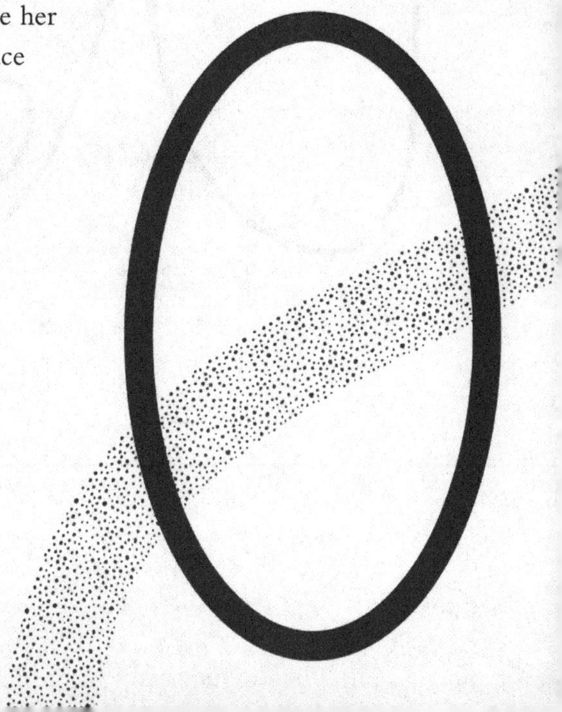

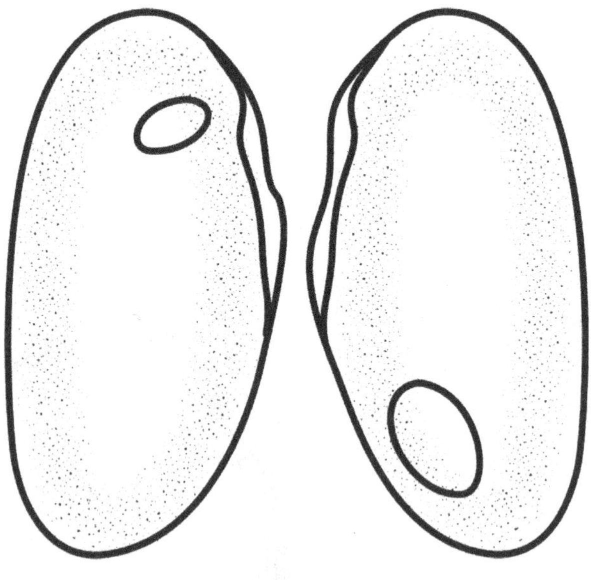

in the before time we
went waist deep
((step)) ((stop))
toed gritty sand on river bend
((stretch)) ((step)) ((stop))
to select smooth-moon-contoured-shells
bent down then
[held our breath]
fingers elongated in longing
for big-mob-feed-full-bellies
((gotcha! Bub, here look))
soaked in fresh water
bathed in garlic butter
grazed pearls on teeth to
test authenticity

((what we had was real))

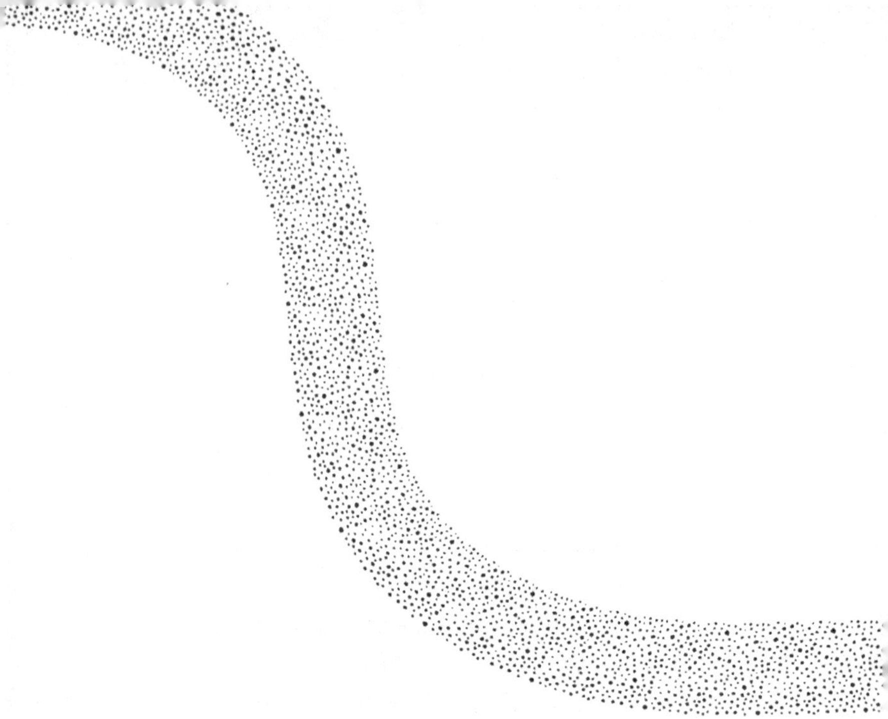

in the before time
you wore the dilly bag
I-wove-you
for corroboree
let bogon-moth-white-ochre
dust from your chest
and set in its ribs as
we orchestrated our own bodies as
| dinawan[1] | mara[2] | ngaran ngaran[3] |
stomping Ngurra[4]
alive with our family's forever stories—
so the long-gone
and the soon-to-come
were all at once
| enshrined |

---

1 emu
2 fish
3 lyrebird
4 Country

in the before time
we spoke our mother's tongues
let~the~mountain~river~and~sea
carry~forward~conversations
and~found~between~us
that fish and
spider and
five and
hand
shared the same name
here and there
and so did
bird

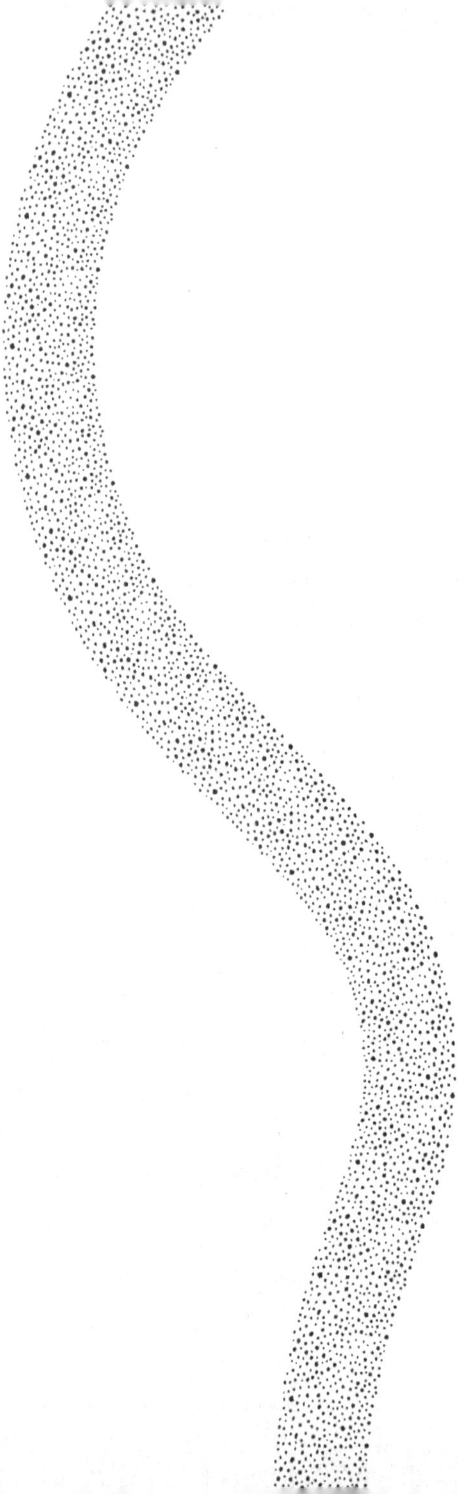

these days
we no longer share sacred
~words~ ((dinner)) | dance | /scars\

our hearts
are no longer
both here and there

our paths
only coalesce and cross

in the before time
~((||/\/\||))~

spiderweb breath
reflective records wind ripple
time skips like scratched soundtrack
staccato ants jut
on mapped tracks
we cannot see
steaming tulsi tea
cloudy peace
settles
magpies serenade the street
a stranger there asks
the hibiscus

if they are always this vibrant
and we just don't see?

I wonder

what else do we miss
for this rushing?

Aunty says
crocodiles hide here

do not be ambushed
by your wandering

| these moments of cool ochre drying | the sun kissing the skin that's left bare |
| the Old People singing with us | with the song men | the babies following our steps |
| the sissies weaving skirts | the Aunties showing us this dance | here look |
| the uncles belly laughing | the littles sharing a feed and playing footy |
| red sauce on everything | the sun setting over the mountain | as full moon rises |
| a vigil | the stories of loved ones long gone but here now |
| the ocean dips to end ceremony | the ochre cloud stirring saltwater |
| the hugs and tears we shed and share then |

| these are the moments |
| these are the moments |

I tell the kids
we saddled megafauna
galloped diprotodon as
if infinite infantry
before we had armies
when there were ice ages
to survive
instead of the colony

They say
AUNTYYYYYYYY
don't be silly

nah true

I tell the kids
we're the Oldest living culture on the planet
that our gadgets outdo iphone-everything
that the Greeks didn't invent it
we did

AUNTYYYYYYYY

nah true

I tell the kids
that before there was royals
there was us

that BC
is supposed to read BK
they meant *before Kooris*

AUNTYYYYYYYY

nah true

I tell the kids
they've got to forget the limitations
they've been set

believe the Elders
before the internet

understand AI
is Aboriginal Intelligence

not falsified fact

AUNTYYYYYYYY

nah true

I tell the kids
baby, just go be you

don't pay much attention to the hearsay
of what they say

stay true
to the sovereignty
flowing through
your veins

stay true
to kinship
and Ancestral ways

stay true
to all you've inherited

uninhibited
by what you heard.

She uses prayer hand emoji to
virtue signal kindness
after cutting words

channel that spirit woman

offer white way ritual
to relieve herself
of the grief she caused

Typical/Ancestral

insert
altar | light | smoke | incantation
an amalgamation of stolen practices
on stolen land
to cleanse the space
(but not her conscience)

already repented today

no need for honesty

ask a foreign God for forgiveness

now a clean slate

all harm washed away
with a text.

psychedelic spinifex
stretch and yawn
mulla mulla fluff
mauve dawn

rosy earth toast
crunch under foot

weatherman ants
scatter
solar

hunting birds hover
suspended in open ended sky
as witness

beneath
the crust

mineral lust
stirs

greed will feed here
again

put hair on the chest of the wealthy

leave
Ngarluma
the crumbs

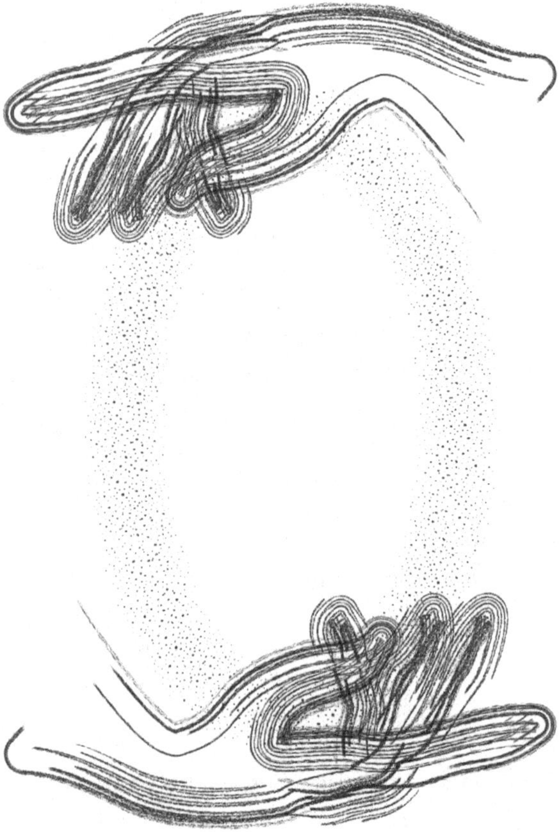

You do not go unnoticed
hand gently slid
between tree skin
and trunk
stick chocks to stretch
synovial blessing
offered with appreciation
from Ancestors

pop
coolamon
and canoe

rub the tree back

soil and ochre elixir

this wisdom is selective
gifted only to the reverent
who can hold it

I see you
cutting
carving
shaping
bending
moulding

wayfinding and carrying forward our future

trust
the Elders chose right
when they chose you

the Elders chose right
when they chose you

sissy songbird let
them hear you

Our Mothers
did not survive birthing blak girls
in sterile suites
for us to sit silent

our Grannies
with mother tongues stapled—
they long for your lungs
to fill and spill out
like Tiddalik
gurgle giggling
the rivers
with their sibling sounds
familial
and understood
beyond the nations and their
mountain bounds

Our mob
redacted

and theirs
and theirs
and theirs

we want your
sacrosanct
serenade

sissy songbird
don't hold out

This city[1] gawks—
morning side eye-lined streets
broken bottle cobble stone paths
homeless peoples' dogs
paid more attention than their owners
the birds paid no attention at all.

This city jams—
acoustic buskers rock out bangers
we can't sing along to yet
because the record company doesn't know
the talent is here
right here
walking namelessly
with thousands of unsmiling others
dodging trams
and fundraising companies'
ambassadors.

This city shudders—
morning commuters move briskly
in joggers,
spare shoes in their backpacks
smart watches
to hold their steps
and keep the time
they'll never get back for this dash
in the name of capitalism
or best case, dharma.

---

1 written on Wurundjeri in loving reverence

This city bike-brake squeaks
creaks and window rattles
with heritage ruling
over re-furb

unperturbed, Birrarung
carves her own way

Wurundjeri and Boonwurrung Dreaming

here to stay
                    forever
          and always.

I escape this city
                              to be
                                        with her.

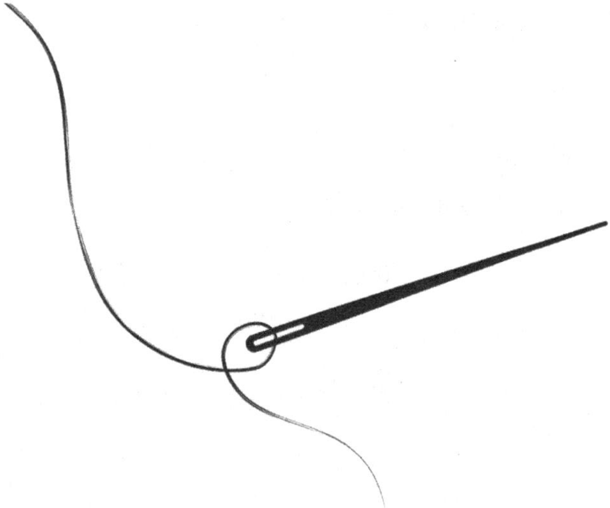

| needles folding through possum skins | Aunty calls this bitch-and-stitch |
| we peel sap from wattle | boil it to make the resin | the kettle sings her readiness |
| time and again |
| black cockatoo flocks kiss the sky above | waves wash the sand white nearby |
| breeze brushes banksia | whistling soft in the daylight |
| no one here whistles at night |
| we know |
| the fire crackles though | she crackles and keeps us close |
| in the cold season |

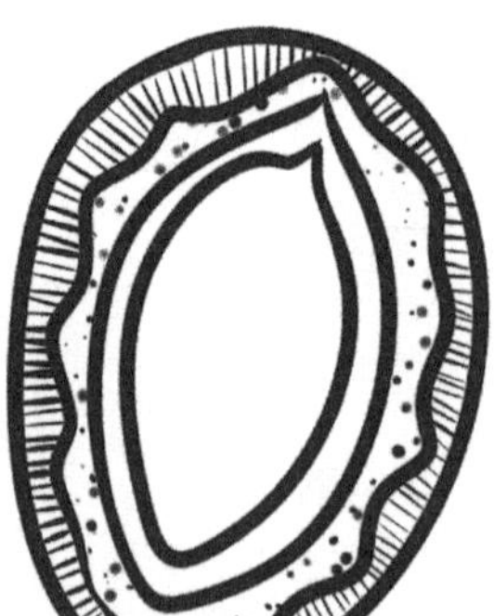

I come from a long line of saltwater women[1]—
Gunai and Yuin on Nan's side,
Biripi and Dharawal on Pop's.

Up and down this coast—we are sea people,

at one with the rhythms of gurawal[2], burri burri[3], muriyira[4],
the whale,
and her calendar flowers

at one with grandmother moon
and her tides

fullest in every sense
when nourished
by Gahdu[5]
with a swim
and a feed.

I learned to separate fishbones from flesh
with my tongue as toddler.

Watched my expert mother elegantly
rock hop, shuck and gulp oysters.

The aunties taught us to pippy dance in
golden sand—
twist and sway.

To harvest and clean abalone
Wulkan[6]

---

1 Originally for Cement Fondue, *Linger Dash Talk* exhibition for World Pride, 2023, also published in *Meanjin*, 2023

2 humpback whale

3 humpback whale

4 humpback whale

5 sea

6 abalone

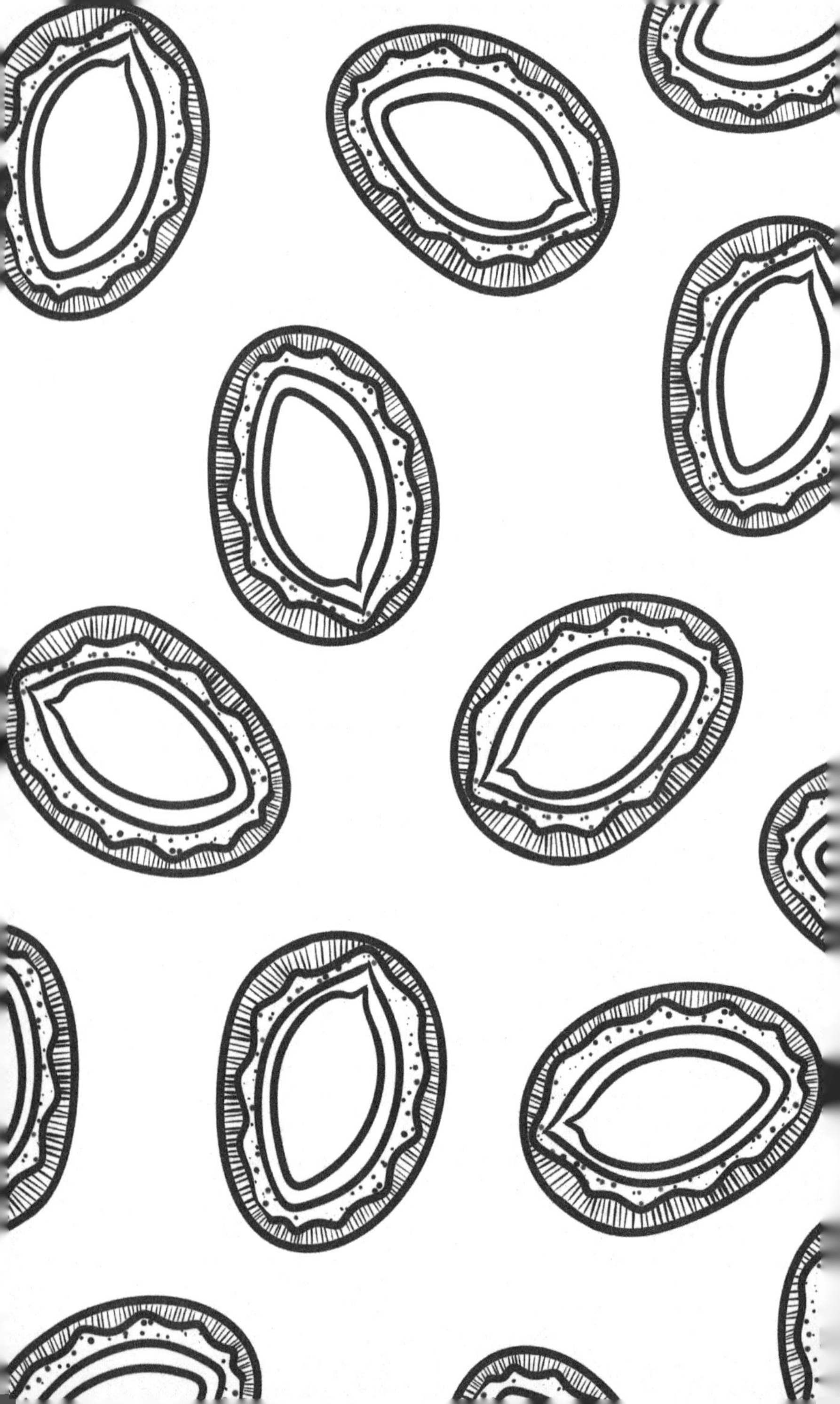

a delicacy for our mob,

to cut away,
gut, and scrub the black on rocks
to beat sweet flesh
to cook over crackling coals
as the sun sets.

They tell me this is Women's Way

and that when Cook came, our fishing changed
in the name of greed,
that what was once abundant and free
was now a commodity
and our people were kept out of the economy
despite being industry leads
in the sea that raised us.

Where abalone are overfished
there are urchins—
thorny black infestations
who feed on the same seaweed and modify reefs with
colonisation
causing barren ground,

so proud aunties can't hand down
this saltwater women's wisdom

and our daughters
at one with the sea

are consumed
in the place we used to feed
by a greed
that longs for sweet
blak-lipped
flesh.

Sis presses cold ochre fingerprints to my skin
marks out Five Islands Dreaming
carefully rounding each one

inherited pattern passed down

cell and story held in land
and now cheekbones

the January air
kilns the clay
feel the pigment
as I move my face
all my emotions crackle dust
leaving a map back to

wide smiles
for the babies who came to ceremony
by the sea for the first time

wide smiles
for the Elders who watch over us
under mountain—
knees no good for dancing now

Sis and I paint the rest of the women up
press handprints for the children—
reminders of their Ancestors
always guiding them
this way this way
come this way

as we become brolga and duck and fisherwoman and whale
sun stains the way around our shapes

tomorrow we'll remember where fingerprints were placed
and always we'll remember how to to paint up this way

cell and story held in land
and now cheekbones

5 deaths in community last week
one a work day
slay

Mob know grief
always a feed
and a bed there for it
welcome it in
like a long-lost cousin

knowing her absence means a
lack of love
or connection

we know isolation is never the answer

so gather
smoke
wail
fill hand with soil
to throw over casket

weave baskets from the hair lost
in the Sorry times

realise as we do

we can hold this too

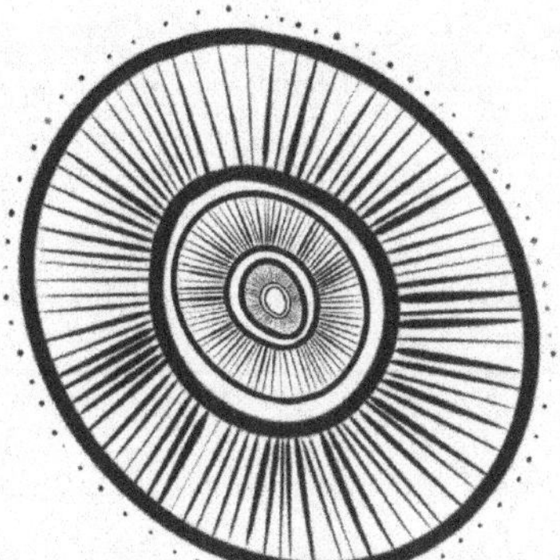

the depths

lustrous
astral travel
sleep in

facetime
surf check
it's clean

we come
undone
in salt water

trance
in torrent

glide
fly
ebb
flow
riptide

symbiosis
osmosis

now
we are oceans

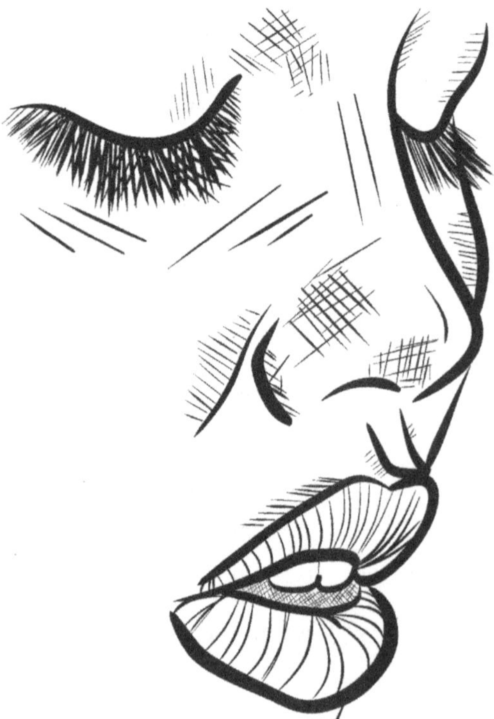

I listen to Queen B on repeat.

Her Lemonade album is this chapter's anthem. I'm a few years behind but this is the glow up I need. This is the black female intuitive reminder of rage and redemption—this is the medicine and the balm.

When she says go call Becky with the good hair[1] I want to send you this song, but we've blocked each other on all the platforms. My only hopes are smoke signals, carrier pigeons and astral travel and let's be honest, you can't sit with yourself long enough to meditate. Right now, you're in another hemisphere driving a mustang, top down, so fast—you'd miss even the most elaborate birds and smoke.

I wonder if our Old People here talk to the Old People there. Maybe they can cheeky DJ hack your spotify playlist like they did mine, queuing up some blak Queens, Aunty Lizzo, Mariah, Aretha, Lauryn. Maybe all the signs and songs about r e s p e c t are simply lost on you.

As I belt out another Beyoncé banger in my pink silk PJs, hairbrush in hand, loving friends on speed dial—I think about that line again. And I hate *her* hair.

Not because your affair partner's hair is particularly good, but because it's not mine and you chose it for months, on the sly, while arriving home through our door moments after cheating, to tell me you love me.

---

1 Beyoncé—'Sorry'

Sorry business would say I cut my own hair now, release you and my strands to the wind, compost and nests made by birds.

Wisdom tells me this pain is rooted, something that cannot simply be cut away. Wisdom says it needs to stay with me a while, so I grow.

When the album ends, I fall to the floor, my stage replaced with rubber and dust.
I find movement.
Stretch 'til my hamstrings are runways.
Salute the sun 'til my shoulders burn.

I find silence on my yoga mat.

There's no pain in presence, and here guided by my young and bendy guru, I return to the teachings of *So Hum*, remembering *I am that*—the oneness we all stem from. Remembering that bodies are just vessels and to hate her hair is to hate my own, is to sow harm into life at large.

Remembering it's not her hair, but your violent hands that pulled it, that I truly cannot stand.

When I close with prayer, my own palms pressed together, head bowed, I ask my Ancestors to send me peace. To help me to forget and better still, forgive. I ask them not to send you that song after all, but another one. Something to keep you true on your path, honest, heart open, aligned with the Ancestors, both of you

—*So Hum.*

do not allow yourself
to be locked out
by the belief
you do not belong

manic
ma~~n~~ic
ma ic
magic

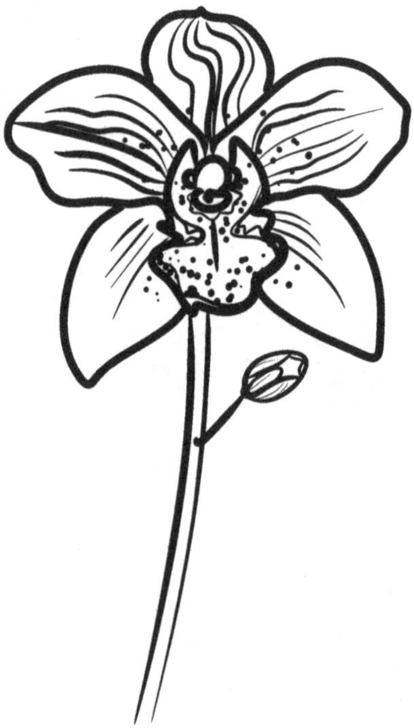

no need to
quarter off cherry chunks
simply to fit in

the glass ceiling
can be reached
and breached
sky high with truth

dissolution is welcome

illusion f/r/a/c/t/u/r/e/d

in healing moments
of full force
when not appeasing
secure in self
in source

satiated wholeness

when taking up space in the world
authentically

Go all in

Go knees scraping
Go spoon licking
'til the bowl is cleaner than we'll ever be despite
our repenting
and relentless bathing in salt water

Go ocean eroded shore
pebbles exposed
and then skimmed on the full moon tide
by hands which don't often take the time to hold the earth

Go flowering gums fireworks
dried in books—so we might find this moment later
when hunting down a poem

Go sparklers conjuring childlike smiles
'til fingertips burn on a wedding night

Go ink on printing press
the kind that won't ever leave your clothes—
remnants of this life work
forever remembered
by a bench who holds the stain

Go painting the architraves
and ceiling together
in a colour no one remembers the name of

Go a love that doesn't know blame
shame or
estrangement
and when you find it

Go all in

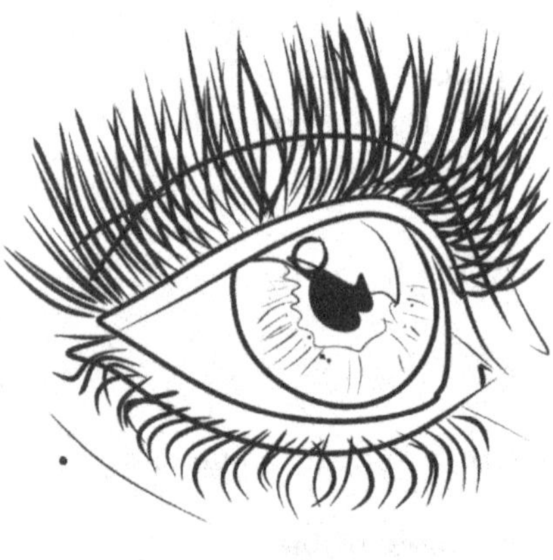

that which is sharpened cuts
smooth
your
eyes
tongue
heart

between the earth and sky we swim
holy middle way

pave the hero's journey
'til one and the same

know the straight and narrow
is devoid
of imagination,
and only hallucinations scatter
offerings here

stray away

take the snake road
long and winding

ripples binding you
with your becoming
'til you're ripe

follow the moon
hot lap the sun
melt, dance and swoon
under yesterday's stars

take as long as you need

be freed from your worries

grow like freeway
wildflowers and weeds

and know
home will be here
when you return

home will be here
when you return

when he asks if I still date men
I tell him

not all men

only the justice minded
who pave the way for change

only those honoring
The Blak Matriarchy

acquainted with the patriarchy
and dedicated to shutting it down

only the strong ones that
know who they are
know where they're from
know where they're going

only the outspoken—
who challenge
gendered violence
shattering silence
with mates
when they cause harm

only the faithful
and the healing

cheeky
affectionate
peace giving

the ones who pour tea
for their Nanny

know what she means
when she says

strong blak sweet

strong
blak
sweet

what should we call this distance between us—

the untouchable midpoint
agony
missing

timeskip
a threshold
the liminal

betwixt transfixed
longing
aching

amid
and among
undone

hopeful
limbo sandwich
the last one

moving on

My crush's friends perch outside
and ripple belly laugh
cackles through the crack
in the window
below herbs and staghorn ferns
shiver on the vibrations
they raise with giggles
in afternoon sun

her messengers plump themselves
ruffle feathers
to shuffle sound around their swirly insides

their message is too big to hide

the spotted gum erupts again
and to the noisy kookaburras I say

go tell her

I wonder if she offers the same
when my birds do fly bys?

hot laps of the dry sky
which the black cockatoos
scour in search of rain to sing in
and freudian slip instead;

call a woman
a storm

echo her name
on escarpment
at sunset
say it again

for the lover who cannot bear to.

constellations

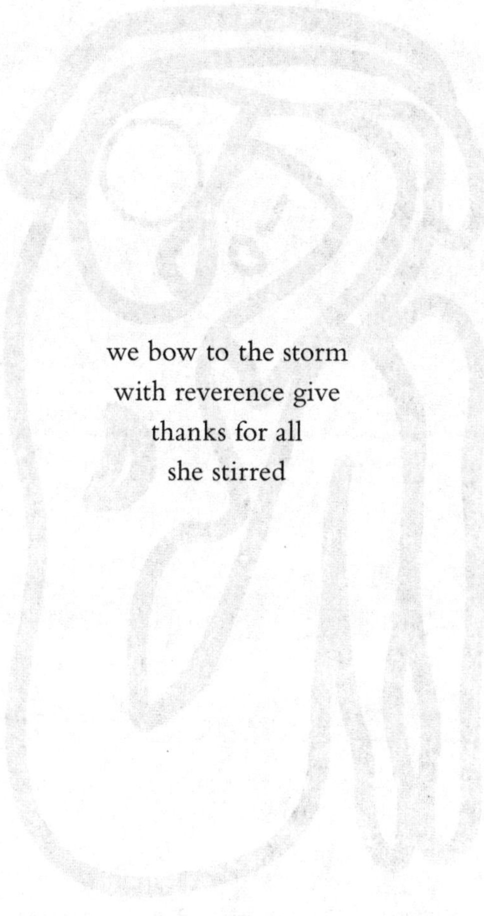

we bow to the storm
with reverence give
thanks for all
she stirred

meteor shower
light show
attention

luminous sun
in opposition to

full moon

intermediary earth
casts shadow

eclipse ellipsis
omit us
from the cosmos
remind us

we were dust once too

change is stirring
beyond comprehension

let the wave crash
on your shore

submerge
deeper and deeper
'til gills grow

in the depths you remember
forgetting is the root cause
of all suffering

fall down the rabbit hole, Alice

destiny is altered
as you observe the melody,
the ethereal of all life

go beyond what is possible

take plenty of friends

bangarang
in the land of the free

transcend duality

chew grace and death with the same teeth

sincerity with tongue in cheek

unapologetically magic,

you, master of letting go.

when Uncle Kendrick[1]
says
we gon' be alright

I hear him
feel him

we gon' be alright

ignite the commute
as I spit along
windows rolled
all the way down

we gon' be alright

celebrate
endemic anthem
of the awakened

we gon' be alright

line my lips
with matte red
villain era
energy

we gon' be alright

incite a riot
of positive affirmation
on my way to work

1 After Kendrick Lamar's song 'Alright'

all of us
alone together
in this

hush-hush
alchemic blush of
quantum physics

where multiple realities exist
and resist
the definitive

schrödinger's cat
alive or dead

the lid still on the box

in this
middle ground
suspension

the tension
of whether this all works out for us is

irrelevant

in our element
when we love like this

unattached
and trusting

unattached
and trusting

BE
ST
FRIE
NDS

Confucius/Bestie says

Gorl, your lover would never keep you guessing
this release is a blessing

let 'em go

when you meet them
you'll know

you know?

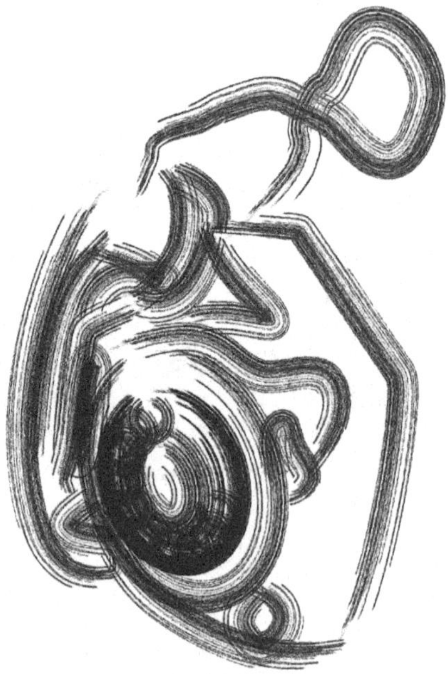

Call me if you ever want to love each other beyond the ~~mother wound~~
Call me if you ever want to love each other beyond the ~~father wound~~
Call me if you ever want to love each other beyond the ~~Ancestral wound~~
Call me if you ever want to ~~love each other beyond the ______ wound~~
Call me if you ever want to swoon in soul healing sacred love

altered states of consciousness
when tapped into the trees

elastic rhythm
bounce us on breeze
like leaves

sunlight of pottered hands
around us as
iris fractal flecks turn
golden

recall us to the specks
we are
in the scheme of things

give us comet vision

give us eagle sight

give us moon eyes
full
and atop
all the worlds
oceans

knead us
in rhythm

with water
and wave

instill in us
Old Ways
and warrior faith

breathe us brave

breathe us brave

this way, come this way, come, this way, come this way, come, this way, come this way, come this way, come, this way, come this way, come, this way, come this way, come, this way, come this way, come, this way, come this way, come this way, come, this way, come this way, come, this way, come this way, come this way, come, this way, come this way, come, this way, come this way, come, this way, come this way, come

defy
G
R
A
V
I
T
Y

. g : a ★ l . a : x - y .
become us

we came for revolution

Blak Matriarchal
- - - centrifugal force - - -

{ synchronised spinning }

the future
^^brimming^^

with the promise of *legacy*
we gave—

we'd leave it better
than it was

_ _ _ when we came _ _ _

...:</?|^[bub, you just keep boogying through the bullshit]^|</>... ...:</?|^[bub, you just keep boogying through the bullshit]^|</>... ...:</?|^[bub, you just keep boogying through the bullshit]^|</>... ...:</?|^[bub, you just keep boogying through the bullshit]^|</>... ...:</?|^[bub, you just keep boogying through the bullshit]^|</>... ...:</?|^[bub, you just keep boogying through the bullshit]^|</>... ...:</?|^[bub, you just keep boogying through the bullshit]^|</>...

if you ever see your lover in another's arms

release yourself the grief

of what you expected
and is now gone

linger in the loneliness
longer

knowing it too will leave

stay

understanding what a privilege it is
to truly miss

there are souls
that never experience

catharsis like this

for spiritual battery recharge
reach out to the river

walk at her pace

no race on
scheduled
go slow days

currents
above
——
below
syncopate

asymmetrical bliss
in tracing
hidden wisdom
within

banks embodied in skin
veins glint
Sky Country reflection

cultivated connection
in remembering

how to simply flow
downstream

keep the homefire
in the belly burning

white smoke circling

warrior women gathering
more powerful together

no transgressor or
oppressor
can harm us here

intuitive union for
collective movement
steeped over tea

sing and sleep sweet

resist while resting

when ready we dance

induce grace to stay
rage against
entrenched misogyny

the system don't know ferocity 'til
it meets

Big Aunty Energy

commune with the divine
find erotic
in the everyday
erode estrangement
unlock the entryway
with meditation
where spirits converge with source
import clarity of this force
flowing freely through you always
remain in this state
as you navigate fate
centre compassion
in place of hate
know universal love
is greater than shame
and find forgiveness
as you erase
what doesn't serve you in
awakened states

when you inevitably meet
the moment
you were taught to crave
ask yourself
do you still?

when night falls
we value light more

carry forth
to what unfolds

the illumination sourced—

the drive
the spark
the unassailable
medicine

found in your
exile

Lorikeet cut through the ether,
mine silence with screech
under coal cliff with black back
dipped in every shade of green,
the trees taller than they should be,
resilient to logging unlike their folks—
red cedars we miss
and speak of in ghostly tongue.

Do you remember when?
Do you remember them?

I do.

Ancestral recall
installed in cells,
Elders tell us
if we misplace
the memory.

I promise to remember
promise to keep the embers glowing,
to stoke the stories
so their sparks fly high
always.

Start spot fires
in our bubbies,
golden ripples of moonlight
on still night
over saltwater

the star ones glittering,
bandicoots mingling
on Dingo Dreaming

the false world
cannot touch us
here.

declare your dreams
court them

circle slowly
wondrously enamoured

grandiose in your romance
loyal to hope

belief unwavering

waft and weave	weld in oneness	we chatter amongst us
fibres, found and forged	from tree and marsh	we make like birds
beak fingers folding	flying	we yarn	here look	try this way
go slower	slower	slower still
sit cross legged on the sand	Sky Country sparkling above
Aunty can't rise so easily now	needs our help to get up
so we stay longer	the littlies watch and rest in the nest of her lap
commit her pattern to memory and dream
the dog at her feet snores

Written for Peace Poetics, on Ngunnawal lands with love for Elfie Shiosaki, Ellen Van Neerven and Natalie Harkin

acknowledgements

Poetry has always been a place of introspection and transformation for me and during 2022–24 I wrote all of these poems for *Eclipse*. It's titled this way because in 2023, when I pitched the book for publishing, the eclipse season in the Sky Country felt unending. And, in my personal life, I had love, heartbreak, grief, great joy, suffering and loss—the full gamut of very human experiences, which seemed to highlight this duality. There were also eclipses of these moments, coming together, which showed me how all of these parts are one and the same.

When an eclipse happens, the world stops to pay attention, and I felt like I was taking stock of my own life while writing these poems, cataloguing moments, so I could put them down to rest, let them go, or write to honour something truly special, kind of like a wordy polaroid.

There's poems in here for my Sissy, encouraging her to sing; for my brother, honouring his art and cultural practice; for my Mum, and a hellish day she'd had at work as a hospital liaison. There are poems for the cheaters, for the women I've had crushes on, for the friends who got me through enormous grief. There are poems for Country, and for the Ancestors.

This collection is playful, it's got a lot more word play than *Returning* or *Kindred*, and I think that's because I was writing music at the same time as making this collection, with my dear friend Mark Chester Harding for our project Cooee (our album also comes out in 2025). It's also full of illustrations, honouring my visual poetry practice, which is probably my favourite way to work—fusing forms.

I hope *Eclipse* brings readers peace, and attunes them to the calm and care of the land, the sea and skies, especially when there is violence and harm and grief, when the world feels wild and too big. I hope it's a grounding, meditative collection that gets carried around and flicked through over coffee, with friends, or on a rainy day when someone has called in sick for work, and is tucked up somewhere cosy, resting. I hope it makes readers feel seen and understood in their experience, that they're not alone in the depths of grief or loss. I hope it feels like a cheeky little beacon, which brightens those moments and celebrates the magic ones too.

That's what these poems have been for me.

And these poems, this collection, wouldn't be possible without my family, friends and community, who inspired the writing, who walked with me in the dark and watched the stars glittering by the fire. Who swam in the ocean and danced beside it with me. Who poured me unending coffee on the window seat at Finny. Who walked with me in the pouring rain and kept me fed and hugged, who painted me with ochre, and who wove and stitched slow. All of you, I love you. Thank you.

Eclipse would also never be possible without the ultimate dream-weaver, the most talented blak editor in the Country, Grace Lucas-Pennington, whose writing inspires me, and who's been with me from the start, with *Kindred*, *Bindi*, *Returning* and now *Eclipse*. Grace, your eagle eyes and wide open heart are so needed in this world, and I'm so grateful to be able to work with you. Thank you for making time.

And thank you, Lillie Paton, my dedicated proofreader, soft editor and all-round creative guru, the Sis who keeps me bubbling with all my creative projects.

Thank you to my mentor for covers and poems and life, Dr Tamryn Bennett, to Brendan Bridgefoot for design tick-tacking, and to Mark, for the musical interpretation of so many of my poems as songs—hearing music when I read now is the greatest treat.

My sincerest thanks too, to my agent, Jane Novak, and the talented publishing team at JOAN, especially Genevieve Buzo, Christa Munns, Mika Tabata and Simon Paterson. Your gentle creative care and patience with this project is so very appreciated. Thank you for all of your dedicated work behind the scenes and for bringing *Eclipse* to the world.

Eclipse was written with the generous support of Creative Australia, who allowed me the dedicated time and collaboration to write, illustrate and edit with this wonderful team. As a full-time freelance artist, this support of process and practice is the stuff of dreams, thank you.

blank space

to hold your poems, love notes, flowers and feathers